T0113242

Kevin Doyle has been a motivational speaker, journalist, entrepreneur, artist, author, publisher, and graduate-school speaker. He lives quite comfortably in Chatham, Massachusetts.

How to Marry Money

KEVIN DOYLE

A PLUME BOOK

PLUME
Published by the Penguin Group
Penguin Group (USA) Inc., 375 Hudson Street,
New York, New York 10014, U.S.A.
Penguin Books Ltd, 80 Strand, London WC2R 0RL, England
Penguin Books Australia Ltd, 250 Camberwell Road,
Camberwell, Victoria 3124, Australia
Penguin Books Canada Ltd, 10 Alcorn Avenue,
Toronto, Ontario, Canada M4V 3B2
Penguin Books India (P) Ltd, 11 Community Centre,
Panchsheel Park, New Delhi – 110 017, India
Penguin Books (N.Z.) Ltd, Cnr Rosedale and Airborne Roads,
Albany, Auckland 1310, New Zealand
Penguin Books (South Africa) (Pty) Ltd, 24 Sturdee Avenue,
Rosebank, Johannesburg 2196, South Africa

Penguin Books Ltd, Registered Offices:
80 Strand, London WC2R 0RL, England

Published by Plume, a member of Penguin Group (USA) Inc.
Previously published in somewhat different form by Doyle Studio Press.

CIP data is available.
ISBN 0-452-28530-5

146119709

Acknowledgments

Thanks are owed to Jessica Bergman, John Jay DeSantis, Deborah Doane, Evelyn Doane, Carolyn Doyle de Batlle, Chappy Greeley, Michael Hale, Jack Hynes, Susan Hayes, Trena Keating, Emily Haynes, John Kelleher, Jenn Mentzer, Julie Saltman, Devin White and Meeghan White.

Contents

Introduction

This lighthearted instruction started out twenty years ago as a series of tongue-in-cheek letters to my daughter Carolyn when she was a fourteen-year-old attending her first coed camp in Vermont.

Years later, when I was holding forth as a book publisher trying to sweeten a midlist with new editions of evergreen titles, I came across copies of those letters and thought they might amuse my attractive and talented young editor, Liz Parker. There was a book in the letters, Liz suggested, if I was interested in developing an instructional text for women who wished to venture forth into the Land of Loot to search for rich husbands. She volunteered to contribute some of the experiences she had heard her friends talk about and had had herself during her courtship with a rich man.

A few years earlier, while advancing her career in publishing, Liz had taken a trip to L.A. and met her future mate at the Beverly Hills branch of the bespoke British shirt store Turnbull & Asser. She'd stopped in to buy a Father's Day gift for her dad.

The Proposition

The examples and instructions herein will show you how to find and marry a rich man. Study this text and you'll be aware of every man in every room you enter. You'll know many things about their backgrounds and pecuniary assets before they even notice the color of your hair. You'll learn how rich men behave, their likes and dislikes. You'll be able to spot phonies. Read this book and you'll not only be aware of these things, you'll be able to act on them. You'll become objective and systematic.

You'll learn to understand your new companions and be a bigger credit to a rich man because you will have a thorough knowledge of his background and an overall grasp of what he is looking for in life. Bid farewell to old routines. You'll be playing a different game. While a heart of gold is important, you will also need a certain amount of old-fashioned ruthlessness. Form your goal. List it; learn it; live it.

If you resolve to marry money, this book will show you how to win the game for keeps.

TOP STORES IN WHICH TO BE SEEN IN THE THREE BIGGEST U.S. CITIES

New York
Paul Stuart, 350 Madison Avenue
Barney's New York, 660 Madison Avenue
John Varvatos, 149 Mercer Street
Thomas Pink, 520 Madison Avenue
Bergdorf Goodman Men's, 745 Fifth Avenue

Chicago
Express Men, 845 N. Michigan Avenue
Davis for Men, 824 W. North Avenue
Public I Ltd., 1923 W. Division Street
Nordstrom, 520 N. Michigan Avenue
Mark Shale, 900 N. Michigan Avenue

Los Angeles
Prada Men's, 343 N. Rodeo Drive, Beverly Hills
Lisa Kline Men, 123 S. Robertson Boulevard,
    Beverly Hills
Scott Hill, 100 S. Robertson Boulevard, Beverly Hills
Hugo Boss, 414 N. Rodeo Drive, Beverly Hills
Faconnable, 9680 Wilshire Boulevard, Beverly Hills

SUCCESS STORY

Bart Evans was a surgeon whose interests included running marathons and hot air ballooning.

Bart was sixty-one, but his net worth of 3.8 million made him seem like a good catch to Whitney, twenty-nine.

The doc appeared to need a woman who understood the demands medicine made on his time and who was willing to play the emotionally supportive role necessary to keep him functioning at full capacity.

This fellow appreciated good food and fine wine, and Whitney's culinary abilities counted for a lot. Though not overly burdened with the green stuff, Whitney had been raised and displayed as a sportswoman in Darien, Connecticut, for the purpose of marrying well. When she was introduced to the doctor at a hospital tennis party in the Rafters Room of Tavern on the Green, Whitney immediately drew the man of medicine in with seductive talk of exotic meals.

Bart had remained single because he believed his hectic life was too unsettling for women he considered marriage material. But Whitney convinced him that he'd found a woman who really understood what it meant to be a surgeon's wife. He would have married her regardless of her education, background, age or any other of those things because, at this stage of his life, social conventions seemed a bit silly, if not altogether superfluous.

Naturally, the whole matter depended on Whitney's ability to lead him to the altar. That turned out to be easier than expected as Whitney was extremely appealing to the eye and sufficiently refined to be at home in the medical circles in which Bart traveled. She appreciated the doc more than the other women he had dated—those who had always been handed the finer things in life on a platter. And it pleased him to be able to give her expensive gifts. Who knew about motives on either side? And who cared?

The doc had a history of maintaining long relationships, and a radiantly happy Whitney eventually made her way down the aisle into the arms of her adoring medicine man.

Having gone and done and kept it up for six years, Whitney now advises girls like you: The best way to attract it is to look and act like you already have it, whether you really do or not.

There are many kinds of men with money. The old and young, the handsome and hideous, the cultured and boorish, the sophisticated and callow, the elegant and rumpled, and the intelligent and stupid may all be numbered among the rich. It would be a pleasant chore to simply choose from this list the qualities that you would prefer in a husband, but your first task is not so easily accomplished. You must first determine what minimum standard of personal qualities would be acceptable to you in a husband. Can you live with an old, unattractive, stupid, vituperative man who is ill groomed and badly dressed? If so, you can probably find a rich one who will marry you. But if you require a man who is matinee-idol handsome as well as rich, your chances will be greatly reduced.

Before beginning your quest for a rich husband, you must determine precisely what grade of man you can attract. If you are overweight and uneducated, your options will probably be limited. But if you can realistically rate yourself as sexy and genteel, your options will be broad indeed. The self-rating process, however, can be excruciating and never fully accurate. Some of us have a deep-rooted predisposition toward self-flattery while others, like the aforementioned Ms. Parker, seem unaware of the elegance they possess even though everyone else sees it. Unfortunately, friends can't always be relied on for an objective perspective either.

There is a less tiresome and more precise method for keying yourself realistically to targets. Simply reflect for a moment on the sort of men that you've been able to attract in the past. Has a handsome, intelligent, good-hearted man ever been interested in you? If so, you will have a reasonable chance with an unattractive, intelligent, good-hearted man. Don't anticipate success with a rich man who also happens to be a dreamboat like your former suitor. If you would prefer not to spend your life with an unattractive man (even if he is rich), you could perhaps settle for a handsome, intelligent, rich scoundrel. A functional system for determining the optimal attributes of a rich man whom you will have a reasonable chance of attracting and reeling in is to list the qualities of the men with whom you've already had a genuine relationship, delete their most endearing qualities, and substitute money. To be realistic, you must set your sights lower when you are on a manhunt and expect to bag a rich one. Don't expect to attract a man who is both rich and desirable in other ways as well. This may be disappointing to hear, but it is nonetheless true.

The advice ahead can give you direction in finding and charming rich men, but no book can impart to you any kind of magic for marrying someone who is an obvious overmatch. No advice can make you significantly more attractive than you already are, and you know best how to make the most of your positive qualities. You are, as Popeye would say, what you are, and you will be recognized for just that. Rich men aren't dopes about taking less than they can have; they understand value and make sure to get it.

Take the above final piece of advice to heart. If you don't, you are likely to hunt, find and fail with a rich target who has been pursued by dozens of women more ruthless and probably just as seductive as you. If you do use what you learn in the following pages, you shall go forth to find, tame and harness a genuine rich man, warts and all.

Who's Who: The Basics

The pedigree of honey
Does not concern the bee;
A clover, any time, to him
Is aristocracy.
　　　　—Emily Dickinson

There are as many kinds of men with money as there are poor men. Personalities range from mannerly reticence to vulgar extroversion. You should consider the various kinds of rich men carefully at the outset of your search and calculate with which type you are most compatible. In other words, for which men will you be able to fulfill the sorts of needs that will lead to a marriage proposal? If your initial assessments are thoughtfully made, you can significantly shorten what is apt to be an arduous prematrimonial program.

How Did They Get It?

Classifying rich men according to the source of their wealth and then describing psychological traits that fit the various classifications is a simple way to deal with a complex subject.

There are two fundamental sources of money: active income earned by work and passive income earned by holdings. Active income is always limited. A dentist can only build so many bridges or a laborer dig so many ditches. Rich men who work and are paid for what they do include corporate executives, professional consultants and recent movie stars. They may have substantial incomes but rarely have they been able to accumulate vast amounts of money. It is the man who has gained a significant income from holdings alone who is really rich.

But it is often more difficult to discover the man who does not need to work for his living than you might imagine. He will often mask his fortune by employing himself in a dabbling or part-time sort of way. If you should notice, for instance, that a man who writes a weekly column in the local newspaper is living in a large house with a heated pool and a nine-car garage, you may assume that his salary from the paper is being supplemented in a substantial manner. It's worth noting that, although you'd expect a man with gratuitous income to invariably have an upper-class background, this is only sometimes the case. He will more often than not be the heir of a lucky real estate speculator, a devious lawyer or a hardworking founder of a chain of dry cleaners.

There are many kinds of fortunes, not all of them

old, not all of them large and not all of them really desirable, but the heir of any fortune will be an entirely different sort of man from one who labors for a living. A working man, even one with a substantial income and luxurious scale of living, will be more dynamic, if more exhausted, and an heir without a career may be more chipper but less forceful.

There is a great distance between an heir whose fortune was generated over a century ago in the China trade and the legatee of a string of car lots in New Jersey, and there will be broad distinctions in personality between men who earn their money in different sorts of employment. Differences are apparent in dress, speech and taste between rich lawyers, nightclub entertainers, airline captains and physicians, but the general stereotypes aren't consistent. Often a man who makes his income in the most mundane way will be more refined than a man whose employment is relatively effete. The owner of a chain of Laundromats may have a taste for symphonic music and quattrocento painting, while a bank president could easily prefer ball games and stock cars. You will have difficulty in accurately assessing the character or tastes of rich men if you consider only the source of their money.

GETTING OUT OF A BAD SITUATION

Bonnie, a friend of Liz Parker, began dating a driven acquisitor after she ran into an old friend from college who dragged her to the Madison Square Garden Horse Show. Though she didn't particularly like horses, Bonnie decided to relax and have a good time. Her seat was next to a man whose two new jumpers were appearing in the show. Bonnie spilled a cup of diet soda into Andrew's lap and mopped it up endearingly while he went on and on about his recent purchase of the horses.

A while into their courtship, Bonnie realized that Andrew's presence at the horse show was a rare moment of relaxation for him; he was supposed to have been on a conference call to Japan, but his Japanese client had canceled the call at the last minute. Andrew usually lived at the office, or on the golf course with clients, or at his home computer pulling up stock performances and other financial information. He canceled plans with Bonnie several times to "close a big deal," and stood her up on her birthday. He was happy to hand her money but had no real interest in how she spent it, whether it was on a gift for him, lingerie (in her eyes, also a gift for him), or a piece of art for that blank wall of his house. Bonnie was beginning to realize that while, yes, she wanted to marry someone extremely wealthy, she didn't want to marry someone who was concerned only with money and accumulating more of it to the exclusion of everything else. The final straw came a day before the wedding, which was to take place on the Maryland horse farm that Bonnie picked out and Andrew purchased for the event.

Bonnie was presented with a one-hundred-page pre-nuptial agreement for signature. The document was so offensive that Bonnie chose to forsake Andrew and his money, and she has now found another man who knows how to enjoy what he has.

How Does He Earn It?

A more insightful way to classify rich men is based on their work and spending habits. External indicators like these can reveal much about the men you will be meeting.

Often a man who harbors the drive to make a lot of money defines his identity and measures his worth or masculinity by the amount of cash he has in the bank or the salary he can command. Corporate ladder climbers and other compulsive workers often disregard the cultivation of personal qualities such as inner strength, courage and honesty that are prized by the hard-pressed lower class and the philosophic upper class. "All that is left for the middle-class man," says New York psychiatrist Dr. Robert Gould, who treats the nouveau riche, "is the battle for the bulging wallets." But exactly what kind of man accepts this monetary way of measuring himself? Gould says, "It is a man with a weak sense of self who doubts his innate ability to attract women. It's hard for such men to face their inadequacies and the anxieties that follow, so they strive for money as a panacea for all their personal ills." Gould's colleague, Dr. Theodore I. Rubin, agrees, saying, "A woman's reassurance doesn't count for nearly as much as business success." An alliance with such a man would obviously have many disadvantages, but if you pay careful attention, you can recognize this flawed personality and avoid men who possess it.

How Does He Spend It?

Another personality that is equally hazardous and to be avoided as much as the driven acquisitor is the aggressive spender, who defines his identity by the way he spends his money rather than by the way he earns it. Linda, a friend of Liz's, was hooked up with such a flamboyant character. The power of his wealth was obvious in everything from the deference of his maid to the dimensions of his limousine. Vulgar objects and vulgar people surrounded him. The ownership of both was flaunted with a tasteless ostentation that could not escape attention. Whatever or whomever he owned had value only for the glory it reflected on him. He would never own a nondescript dog, and none of his human entourage, including Linda, was less than de rigueur either. His sensitivity to the pleasurable rapport one could feel with certain people was entirely undeveloped; he used people around him only to flatter himself or to intimidate strangers. On those occasions when his lavishness extended to giving Linda gifts, his presentations were made in a way that rubbed her nose in his generosity, and he never explained what had inspired the gift in the first place. As a result, Linda felt as if she was a possession, not a girlfriend. It was obvious that he was only interested in her as long as she kept quiet and looked pretty—when it came down to it, she was just another accessory to him, a beautiful piece that once again proved to the world that he could have anything he wanted.

But Linda, an expert sailor, found her luck changing when she took a position as a skipper on an oceangoing sloop. Her new suitor, the boat owner's son, hung around the helm until Linda accepted his well-bred hand in matrimony. "Marriage can be a man's chance for social elevation, but for women the opportunity is usually of an economic nature," states the pixyish yachtswoman, now thirty-two and celebrating eight years of marriage following an Easthampton wedding and Bermuda honeymoon.

Linda's favorite quote is from former United States treasurer Ivy Baker Priest, who said, "Why should we mind if men have their faces on the money, as long as we get our hands on it?"

The Alternatives

If you can steer clear of the two kinds of rich men described above, the driven acquisitor and the aggressive spender, you will have averted some opportunities for disaster. Unfortunately, money and its corrupting power does affect most rich men to some degree and you will encounter still other types who, while not as obviously distasteful, should be avoided just the same. But you can find rich men, as Bonnie, Liz and Linda have, who will make tenable husbands and who may even become better adjusted to the world around them despite their money as a result of having a relationship with a woman like yourself. These are the rich men to pursue. These are the rich men you can marry.

A common type of rich man who may need you most is one who feels guilty about his inheritance. The man who has inherited a great deal of money is often beset by feelings that much of his success and popularity are the result of someone else's good fortune and not of his own doing. He is tentative and conservative, never the frisky dispenser of easy money and good times. What a man like this needs is a new positive vision of his own self-worth. Being supportive and offering encouragement to a man like this may help him blossom magnificently, in turn helping you to bring your dream of walking down the aisle with him to fruition.

Another kind of rich personality develops from the pressures of the extraordinary opportunities that accompany inherited money. A man who doesn't need to work and has not been able to find an involving avocation often feels useless. He lives with a need to prove himself because his inheritance has precluded the necessity of a job that engages a working man's energies. Heirs often cannot take on the role of strong provider or courageous survivor to lend credibility to their masculine personalities. It's all been done for them.

There is a large range of responses to the problems of an existence without a meaningful career challenge. Men with some talent may become artists or scholars or sportsmen, and even without distinguishing themselves greatly may develop a satisfactory self-image. Others will train for a profession but practice only in limited ways. Still others, usually young, will disassociate themselves from their inheritances in order to avoid overpowering expectations (both their own and those of others) of spectacular success and self-fulfillment. If one begins from a privileged position and sets out with all of the necessary resources to excel, to not do so may feel like a great failure. The counterculture of the sixties and the seventies was a convenient haven for many of these conflicted young heirs. The idea at the time that the establishment and money were "bad" allowed many young people the luxury of languishing and not living up to the expectations that accompanied their good fortune.

If a man has not completely alienated himself from his family, this heir-without-airs can often return to a life of comfort and can, at the same time, due to his democratic attitudes, remain accessible to people "beneath his station." He may always retain quirks from his honorable days of self-sufficiency and insist on driving an old Saab or on burning wood instead of oil. But if you can manage to steer him in the direction of starting a family of his own, his instincts as a provider will soon overcome his rebellious streak and your style of living should gradually move toward that which you are hoping to become accustomed. You may even find yourself launched into a world of whimsical luxury, which is, after all, the legitimate habitat of your adventuresome new partner.

At the other end of the chronological and psychological spectrum is the rich man of earlier vintage. If he has always been rich, he's probably led his life thus far in the pursuit of pleasure, doing whatever he wishes whenever he wishes. His goal is to always feel at ease and be in control, and he is often drawn to younger women who allow him to maintain such a position in relationships. However, this is a seasoned man of means and one who is quick to spot mercenary motives. Candor on your part is your best bet. With honesty, of course, comes danger—you should make certain at the outset that your prospect is worth it. His assets should be commensurate with those that you are ultimately looking for in a husband.

If on a first date your escort constantly drops names and labels over dinner, he's probably making just as big an effort to pretend he has a lot of money. Women as phony as he is will pretend they don't want any of it, but you would be better served insisting on proof of what he really has in the bank.

The Pretenders

There are many clues that can help you discover the magnitude and quality of a man's fortune. You need not be misled by a few external signs of wealth, nor discouraged by their absence. To accurately gauge a man's wealth, you must first assess whether he is a recent arrival to the Land of Loot. This can be accomplished best by close observation of his clothes and, if possible, his house.

The clothes of a man with new money will look new. They will be cut in the most recent style from cloth that the fashion magazines have deigned "in" and "hot," and they will never show signs of use. The new-money man will wear them as self-consciously as a poodle in ribbons, never letting you forget that they are expensive and considered chic. On the other hand, a man who grew up rich and was required to wear a tie and jacket in grammar school will wear clothes of the same traditional style all his life. Some will show signs of wear and they will always be worn unassumingly. In other words, he wears his clothes, they don't wear him.

The house of a newly rich man will also be new and filled with expensive art and furnishings. Often, one or both of his city and country houses will be condominiums.

The old rich also usually have more than one house, but each will be stately and imposing enough to appear to have been built before his great-great-grandfather was born. He will have one in town for the winter, one in the country for the summer and sometimes one on foreign soil just for the hell of it.

In addition to learning to discern between men of new and old money, you must also learn to recognize at a glance a man who is simply pretending to be any kind of rich. Behind the gold Dunhill buttons of a habitual blazer wearer you are certain to meet many of the wrong types. The Poseur is in love with himself. The Playboy or Wannabe will tell you anything to get you into bed. The Climber will use you to get ahead himself and, once there, kick you to the curb. The Creep is eager to lead you into some nightmare that could be degrading, dangerous or both.

Exaggerated arrogance, charm laid on too thick, flamboyant spending, an Italian wardrobe (acceptable only in the entertainment industry), monogrammed everything, name- and/or label-dropping and, yes, capped teeth are some of the more salient red flags that indicate a phony who is working it as hard as he can. Two or more of these indicators coupled with an ostentatious automobile and an invitation to sleep over on a second date are sure certification of a shallow and witless pretender interested only in the most desperate and depressing of all human encounters: the one-night stand or a very short fling in which the only one who comes out a winner is himself.

Generally speaking, a man with a Mercedes is less

likely to be a phony than one in a BMW, and the handsome stud with the Omega is more apt to be solvent than the one with the Rolex. A single man is more apt to have both feet on the ground if they're shod by Church or John Lobb than Bruno Magli or Gucci, and more apt to be the genuine article if his shirt is from Thomas Pink rather than Versace. The really rich are more likely to bound out of bed early in the morning with a "Hello, world" attitude and answer their phones on the first ring. Fringe characters often screen their calls and conduct business (whatever that "business" might be) in the evenings.

Occasionally you will spend time with a man who has many of the accoutrements of wealth but leaves you uncertain as to whether he really is what he claims. When a light moment arrives, ask him offhandedly if he is rich. If he answers, "That depends what you mean by rich," he's most likely a fake.

TARGET PROFILE
The Attorney

Age: 31
Height: 5'10"
Weight: 175 lbs.
Interests: Golf, horseback riding and court tennis
Net Worth: $1.7 million

Mr. Hustle seeks a woman who fits in at the country club and mixes well with his clients. A lawyer's wife must realize business will come as much from social contacts as professional ones.

He admires strong women who aren't afraid to take risks, but he must have someone with the look of a conventional corporate wife. For ambitious lawyers, especially those looking to make partner or stay one, you must be willing to look the part, dressing in a conservative style and perhaps wearing nylons with everything except your tennis dress. Be quiet but sharp. And the ability to mix a martini he can boast about can't hurt.

The Attorney sample Q&A

Q. *Why are you still single?*
A. What's the hurry?
Q. *What is your type?*
A. I like women. Period. Names, ranks and serial numbers aren't important. Her background and credentials don't matter to me. Don't misunderstand me, however. The woman I marry must look the part of a successful

attorney's wife, and she must be able to handle herself well at a client dinner for four as well as at a gala event for four hundred. Wackiness was cute when I was at Choate, but no more. Even if I was attracted to that kind of woman now, I'd never marry her. I want someone who will fit in with the prescribed lifestyle. I've got the right condominium, the right car and I want the right woman. She can be from Brooklyn, but her looks and attitude have to scream Grosse Pointe.

Q. *Under what circumstances would you marry?*

A. When I meet the woman every attorney would want for a wife.

Q. *How long have your previous relationships lasted?*

A. From hours to years.

Q. *Do you engage in more than one relationship at the same time?*

A. I refuse to incriminate myself.

Q. *How do you meet women?*

A. By introducing myself at work-related events, wedding receptions and cocktail parties.

The Upper Class

I've been rich and I've been poor.
Believe me, honey, rich is better.
—Sophie Tucker

As in every other country around the world, the highest social class in America has a great deal more than just money. They have a long, often colorful history of having money. A bona fide patrician American family can trace its origins back along a gilded path for eight or ten generations to colonial beginnings of dubious virtue. These people grow up, go to school and marry among themselves. They live in a world apart that is difficult to penetrate.

You shall almost certainly be excluded from this group. But it is important for you to have detailed knowledge of the nature of this society because the people to whom you do have access, the affluent bourgeoisie, the professionals, the new rich and so on, all try to model their own tastes and manners on the older, more traditional society.

wealthy will endure morbidly predatory jungles, impossibly frigid mountain peaks or ruthlessly arid deserts.

The members of the most upper of classes are also ready to demonstrate self-reliance in ways other than deft management of physical circumstances. They usually skipper their own yachts (even the largest) and pilot their own planes (even the fastest). They often cook and garden expertly. They are not intimidated by large dogs and are ready, especially the young girls, to rein in and show statuesque horses.

The same hearty self-assurance that enables the upper class to endure the rigors of the activities above is also at the heart of their notorious talents for enjoying themselves. The old rich will take their pleasure wherever and whenever they find it. They completely lack the obsessions of the middle class with regard to fashion or status. The upper class, in a simple, uncluttered and enjoyable way, embraces the very heart of a pleasurable experience. No mock alpaca golf sweaters hang festively in the wardrobes of the upper class; they feel no need to adorn themselves in certain ways in order to announce an intention to relax.

The most boisterous of upper-class fun lovers were, for a long time, the postadolescents. They had the money and energy to use their recreational resources to the fullest. They got a kick out of crashing sleek automobiles and were thrilled to go swimming in evening clothes. People loved them and their joyful ways or hated them and their profligacy. But there has been, in recent years, a new attitude among a portion of the young rich that has precluded all sorts of privileged romping. These young members of the old society have systematically rejected the habits and values of their forebears and adopted instead a laughable affectation of swaggering independence. They have lowered themselves to all sorts of oddly demeaning positions, such as being sycophants to tradesmen or hangers-on to drug dealers. You can probably capture one of these poncho-wrapped traitors as easily as you might marry an impostor in white tie and tails, but there will still be no money for you. Excessively rebellious rich kids have usually been disinherited completely or are subsisting on punitively constricted allowances or trust funds. You should disregard the aberrant behavior of these young turncoats in trying to understand the true nature of the real upper class, but do keep in mind that it really does exist.

In addition to the disaffected youth, there are many atypical members of the upper class. Well-connected eccentrics are probably more bizarre than the more modest deviants among the lower classes, and their antics are certainly much more publicized. But you must not focus on the oddities of the class—instead focus on the true-blue qualities of the old rich. These graceful paragons are the models that are carefully studied by the affluent bourgeoisie and the new rich.

Q. *How long have your previous relationships lasted?*
A. About a year. Four months of rapture, four more of doubt and then four of pain and confusion.

   I had a fling a year or so ago with a college girl. She was young and bright, and I thought she was going to expose me to new places and people—maybe even new emotions. But it turned out that she was really only after cheap thrills. Expensive cheap thrills.

Q. *Do you engage in more than one relationship at the same time?*
A. I'm a sentimental loyalist.

Q. *How do you meet women?*
A. Usually by colliding with them in the fast lane.

Where the Rich Boys Are

Let me smile with the wise and feed with the rich.
—Samuel Johnson

If you're presently circulating in social circles that encompass rich men, the task of meeting one of them becomes, of course, much easier. If rich men are not regularly included in your circle, you must develop active programs to make contact. Don't squander time waiting for one to come along.

There are two paths to take in the active search for rich men. The first path will lead you into a maze of social contacts with people who have the ability to introduce you to rich and available men. The second, more direct route is to discover the names and addresses of unmarried rich men and then develop a plan that will give you an opportunity to introduce yourself to one, and then to another.

The first method, which relies on conventional social contacts, can be extremely frustrating and time-

KILLING TWO BIRDS WITH ONE STONE

Spas are not for everyone, but if you can afford it, you might want to think about booking a trip to one that provides plenty of healthy food, exercise and lifestyle activities.

Here are four outstanding coed spas where you can get into shape while meeting plenty of rich men:

Canyon Ranch, Tucson, AZ, and Lenox, MA
(1-800-742-9000)

Golden Door, Escondido, CA
(1-800-424-0777)

Miraval Life in Balance Resort & Spa, Tucson, AZ
1-800-232-3969

Rancho La Puerta, Tecate, Baja California, Mexico
1-800-443-7565

SUCCESS STORY

"I couldn't support myself in the manner to which I'd grown accustomed and neither could anyone I was meeting. I'd been divorced for five years and was at the end of my rope when I met John," states Arlene, an accountant, who at forty looks and acts ten years younger.

While backing her aged roadster out of the parking lot after a polo match at the Myopia Hunt Club, a big green Mercedes turned in and demolished her trunk and taillight. The driver was a partner in a large Boston law firm, and he apologized effusively, insisting Arlene go back inside with him to recover from her jolt. After John excused himself from his cronies at the bar, a languorous dinner at a corner table ensued, and it was quickly evident that there was a mutual attraction between the two.

"John liked the idea that I was independent and could work autonomously with figures. And I suppose my own figure had something to do with it too," Arlene admits. "After three months he proposed, and I accepted in three seconds."

Arlene's advice is to see opportunities even in the middle of disaster. "If I'd acted as bitchy as I was feeling that day in the parking lot, I wouldn't be where I am today."

Try sailing to one of the private offshore islands that line both U.S. coastlines. Shipwreck yourself and get rescued by a sailor, preferably one named DuPont, Forbes, Fisher, Gardiner or Simmons. Once on dry land, make your own moves for the rest of the summer and, if you're not engaged by Labor Day, return to the city . . . and hit those Social Registers and phone books!

consuming. What you will actually be doing, for the purest of motives, is social climbing. This is an activity fraught with pitfalls and one that will expose you to more treachery and insult than you can imagine.

If you ever do manage to penetrate the inner sanctum, you will be less than halfway to your goal, because the matrons who run the more affluent social circles guard their bachelor pool jealously and nothing is more disappointing than to lose an "extra man" to someone outside their circle. The other ladies of the circle, old and young or married and single, will rigorously insulate any eligible men, keeping you from making contact. And the younger, unmarried women will devise plenty of poisonous programs to doom your matrimonial intentions.

Many months or years can be wasted in vain attempts to navigate the waters of the upper class, however rich they may be in matrimonial treasure. Unless a convenient opportunity arises to go cruising in them, you would be wise to focus your energies into more direct channels.

Always remember: good fortune is more likely to arrive when the welcome mat is out. To be effective in your search, it is necessary to be specific. You must have a clearly defined idea of the particular type of man you are looking for and then pinpoint names and addresses. The preceding chapters have helped you learn which type of rich men present realistic opportunities for marriage, but you cannot simply go about your daily routines waiting for one to cross your path. You must find out who the rich, single men are in your community. Once you have developed a list of names and addresses, you have made the first in a series of steps that leave nothing to chance and will produce results. In larger cities, it is simple to begin such a list by using the Social Register, an annual directory of men and women who comprise the most elite social circle of the community. In New York City the list occupies nearly one thousand pages. Social Registers are published for several of the large cities in the United States, including Washington, D.C., Philadelphia, Chicago, Boston, St. Louis, Pittsburgh, Cleveland, Cincinnati, Dayton, San Francisco, Baltimore and Buffalo. They are published by, and may be obtained through, the Social Register Association, 381 Park Avenue South, New York, NY 10016.

As well as first and second home addresses with telephone numbers, the Social Register will include information on where and when a man attended college, his occupation and, if he has a wife, her maiden name. Everyone in the Social Register will have social connections of one sort or another, but not all of them have money. The Social Register can help in finding men who are more likely to be rich, but inclusion in the Register is not a guarantee of wealth.

If no list is published for your city or town, there are alternatives for initiating organized expeditions. Additional steps are involved, but you should be able to generate a strong list of wealthy prospects.

You can pinpoint rich professionals by looking in the yellow pages under the listings for attorneys, physicians, stockbrokers and dentists—then cross-checking the white pages to find their home addresses. The names that have fashionable addresses are the ones you want. The next step is to call his home, and disguised as a market researcher for a cosmetics company, ask for Mrs. McBucks. If you're speaking to Mrs. McBucks, move on. But if a housekeeper answers and informs you that there is no Mrs. McBucks, you are on your way. The next step is to find a reason to stop by your target's office or home to check him over. If he looks like a possibility, you can proceed using the tactics outlined herein.

Another way to locate rich men is to find out who owns the larger and more profitable businesses in your town. You may be able to do this through the Chamber of Commerce or by calling the main office of the local department store, contracting firm, manufacturer and so on, and finding a reason to ask for the owner. Many of the rich men you meet will be married, but some will be available, and if you invest even just a few days' effort, you will discover a few desirable prospects.

A more random, less organized approach to finding rich men is to go to the places where they spend their time. A woman with poise and confidence can walk into the VIP lounge at any airport, into an auction for expensive antiques or into the crowd of spectators at a polo match, and no one will bat an eye. You can easily find a real estate broker to take you through expensive houses and, in some, the owner's possessions will be on display, giving you an idea of just how much he's worth. Get your name on the invitation list for museum and gallery openings. Not everyone will be male or rich, but some will be both.

If you hear about a school reunion or benefit, don't be reticent about attending uninvited. As with the airport VIP lounge, if you act like you belong there, people will think that you do.

Don't, however, be as overeager as wide-eyed Grace, now thirty, who met a seemingly perfect man using exactly the method above. Grace simply walked into an airline VIP lounge at one of the New York area's major airports, figuring it was worth seeing what would happen. She wasn't sitting with her drink for more than five minutes when a man who turned out to be as charming as he was handsome approached her and starting chatting. He had been doing business in Manhattan and was taking a flight home to Chicago that night (first class, of course), but could they have dinner the next time he was in town? Grace was totally swept off her feet, and thus started their long-distance relationship: he called her from Chicago and saw her every time he was in the New York area, usually arriving at the apartment he had rented her in the city with some

Kansas
  Shawnee Mission

Kentucky
  Indian Hills

Louisiana
  New Orleans Garden District
  Bayou Liberty

Maryland
  Annapolis
  Northwest Baltimore
  Roland Park

Massachusetts
  Chestnut Hill
  Dover
  Hamilton

Michigan
  Bloomfield Hills
  Grosse Pointe Farms

Minnesota
  Edina
  Lake Minnetonka
  Wayzata

Missouri
  Clayton
  Ladue

New Jersey
  Basking Ridge
  Far Hills
  Short Hills

New York
  Bronxville
  Locust Valley
  Pound Ridge

North Carolina
  Chapel Hill
  Pinehurst

Ohio
  Gates Mills
  Pepper Pike
  Waite Hill

Oklahoma
  Nichols Hills
  Southeast Tulsa

Oregon
  Lake Oswego

Pennsylvania
  Bala Cynwyd
  Bryn Mawr
  Fox Chapel
  Wynnewood

Rhode Island
  Barrington
  Newport
  Watch Hill

South Carolina
  Charleston (north of Broad)
  Aiken

Texas
  Highland Park
  River Oaks
  University Park

Virginia
  McLean
  Middleburg

Washington
  Bellevue
  Kirkland
  Mercer Island

Washington, D.C.
  Foggy Bottom
  Foxhall Road
  Kalorama

A resort church group (particularly in summer en-
claves of old money along the Atlantic coastline) is used
to visitors in the congregation and you might find it
easier to get in touch with the local single men if you
try attending services in one of the places like the following:

Hobe Sound, Florida
Mt. Desert, Maine
Nantucket, Massachusetts

Analyze just what your resources are. Are you intelligent? Beautiful? Do you have any upper-echelon acquaintances? Do you have a substantial amount of
venture capital? Do you look good in a bathing suit?
Are you an exceptional tennis player or horseback
rider? Do you sail? Do you know about painting or
sculpture? Do you speak a foreign language? Do you
play baccarat or backgammon?

After clearly identifying your most promising assets,
choose a favorable setting for them. If you have a great
body, go where you can spend eighteen hours a day in a
bikini. If you are fluent in French, visit Paris. If you
have a friend who's rich or looks rich, travel with her.

Learn where the rich men from your locale tend to vacation. It's a lot easier to keep the relationship going when the man is from your hometown. Read social columns for the location of resorts, cruises or charter boats on which you might take an adventurous jaunt.

If you pick as your quarry a rich guy who likes fishing, try to determine what tempts him the most before you present the bait. Remember that, in this pastime, form seems to count for more than a creel full of the finny fellows. Learn about trout stream etiquette. When speckled trout rise in the mountain streams and the scent of lilacs tease the memories of gentlemen anglers, a knowledge of brook entomology, for instance, could serve you well, along with an ability to tie a tan caddis pupa.

Contrivance is the key to meeting men at their leisure. Assess your hotel. Learn if guests regularly use the dining room or venture off the hotel grounds. After a few days in a hotel environment almost everyone is open to new acquaintances. If there is only one rich bachelor in such a place, you will be sure to meet him without seeming pushy at all. In travelers' hotels or resorts the atmosphere is less intimate so you will have to extend yourself to meet a prospect. On the other hand, you will have more prospects.

From November, when roses linger on in England's misty green countryside, until April, when they bloom again, you can follow the fox in the timeless shires north of London. Stay at Hambleton Hall, a Victorian hotel in the heart of Leicestershire's hunting country. It's the perfect headquarters in which to set yourself up to meet rich men who attend such famous hunts as the Quorn, Cottesmore and Belvoir. Any British innkeeper will help you.

Ride to the hounds or sniff out the scent of British sterling in villages with stately hedges and dry stone walls. Whatever your fortune following the fox, you'll come home well steeped in the rites of old money.

Whenever possible, schedule your entrance into a dining room to coincide precisely with the arrival of your quarry. As you both wait for the maître d'hotel, try one or more of the following: tell your target you admire his suit, tell him his tennis game or crawl is impressive, or that his cigarette holder or pinkie ring is very elegant. Break your too-high heel; ask for a match. Do anything to make contact. You must act without hesitation in this situation. No man wants to dine alone and your pretext is sure to lead to an invitation. If you lose your nerve, let the maître d' do the talking for you. Simply stand close to your target, facing him with a smile as the maître d' approaches. The maître d' will assume you are together and say, "Table for two, monsieur, madame?" Just keep smiling, as if you understand nothing. If the gentleman acknowledges the mistake, insisting that you take the first table, be generous and cordial, saying, "Why don't you sit at my table? Dutch treat. . . ." If, on the other hand, he is impolite enough to take the first table, then follow him and there will be such confusion when you all converge at the appointed table that he will have to acknowledge your presence and say something. That should be just the opening you need.

Another trick: If, after a careful and unobtrusive surveillance of your intended, you've found him in a theater seat, on a deck chair, on a bar stool or reclining poolside on a chaise longue—stand by and wait for him to leave for a moment. As soon as he leaves, scoot in and take his place, regardless of whether he has secured the spot with a drink, book or towel. The more outrageously inept your appropriation of his space has been, the more effusively self-deprecating you can be in your apologies when he returns, and the deeper he will be drawn into his own apologies for making you uncomfortable. His only mannerly option may be an invitation for you to remain. He could wind up right in your lap . . . literally!

A sportsman is always vulnerable. Fun-and-game events provide dozens of pretexts for establishing contact. In sporting situations, you or your team members can make all sorts of mistakes that will require his gentlemanly understanding. If he plays tennis, notice his brand of tennis ball and buy the same for yourself. Take a neighboring court and scoop up his errant balls, insisting they belong to you. Be dogmatic. Make him prove his rights. If he shows you a symbol on one of the balls that proves possession, take that one too. After being completely clueless and bitchy, relent—the least you can do in apology is invite him for a postcourt refreshment.

Opportunities

With these thoughts in mind, let's begin the business of seeking opportunities for you in the matrimonial marketplace.

The cardinal virtues (justice, prudence, fortitude and temperance) are simple standards to live by in your quest for love, glory and financial elevation. Virtue alone, though, is unlikely to bring you the rewards you seek. You must actively pursue your goal and recognize opportunities, making the most of them when they come your way.

If you own a dog, walk him or her in the best neighborhoods. If your sweet little poodle should do something as disastrous as bite a rich man you've had your eye on, do what Suzie did when her pet nipped a customer in a Mercedes showroom in Grosse Pointe: She stepped right in to administer first aid. Now she's raising their kids and several more dogs.

Smile a lot. You look prettier and easier to approach. Don't hesitate to make eye contact with well-groomed targets.

Try this one a few times. Sit down next to that interesting-looking chap in the lobby of an expensive hotel and begin to thumb slowly through your well-worn copy of a Louis Malle screenplay. He's likely to be impressed with your tasteful choice of reading material, and chances are he'll strike up a conversation. This tactic will also work well in the first-class section of an airplane.

TARGET PROFILE
The Heir

Age: 37
Height: 5'11"
Weight: 175 lbs.
Interests: Hiking and publishing lifestyle books
Net Worth: $8.6 million

His interests are varied so it's hard to say what type of woman the heir will respond to. She could be a whimsical sprite who is a bit off-kilter and shares his charitable concerns, or a steadfast entrepreneur with money of her own.

This fellow is not nearly as perfect as he seems at first, and he may need to draw strength from you to deal with his feelings about the fact that money is just handed to him, that he doesn't need to make money on his own.

The Heir sample Q&A

Q. *Why are you still single?*
A. Destiny has thus far denied me a suitable mate.
Q. *What is your type?*
A. One who stirs my heart and enriches my soul.

It seems I've always been able to pick and choose from a large but not particularly varied group of women. But for the past five or so years, I've been circulating beyond friends of the family or friends of friends. In other words, I've been dating women of a different social class.

I've always tried to be open-minded and have been somewhat active in philanthropic causes. But now, for the first time, I'm really seeing how things are outside my narrow circle. The lives of some of the women I've been spending time with lately are exciting to me. Many seem as though they're living on the edge and, though it would probably sound improbable to those who know me, I'm looking forward to dating women who can broaden my horizons.

Q. *Under what circumstances would you marry?*

A. If I found someone with whom I could establish a common strength and hope.

Q. *How long have your previous relationships lasted?*

A. Relationships are never over. They just become less active as ardor fades.

Q. *Do you engage in more than one relationship at the same time?*

A. Not if I can help it.

Q. *How do you meet women?*

A. Most of my friends are married now, but they always have unattached women around when they entertain. More recently, I've met women through my charity work and now and then at gallery openings.

THE ONE SIGNATURE ACCESSORY
YOU NEVER SEE (OR SAW) HER WITHOUT

Queen Elizabeth—Hat
Jacqueline Kennedy Onassis—Oversized sunglasses
Barbara Bush—Pearls
Lily Pulitzer—Pink and green fashion
Princess Caroline—Helga Wagner necklaces
Hilton Sisters—Paparazzi
Babe Paley—Long black pearl cigarette holder
Dina Merrill—Chanel bag
Clarie Booth Luce—Jack Rogers sandals

Putting Your Best Foot Forward

Fortune and Love befriend the bold.
—Ovid

Rich men appreciate many different kinds of women, but they are likely to marry one kind only: ladies. Fortunately, in contemporary times, many sorts of behavior are deemed sufficiently ladylike.

There are a few paragons of traditional etiquette strutting around in designer jeans these days, but there is still a distinguishable difference between someone who is shaking it with class and someone who is not. In all circumstances you must sustain a dignified, as well as appealing, aura about you. The first step in doing this is to familiarize yourself with the traditional forms of genteel behavior, either by attending finishing school or, for those saving money to go to a resort once armed with all of the necessary tools, by reading one of the classic books on etiquette. The volumes by Amy Vanderbilt and Emily Post cover this material in depth, but you should not necessarily mimic the priggish behavior they recommend for unmarried ladies. You should merely have a familiarity with the standards that Mmes. Vanderbilt and Post advocate so that your own deportment reflects the earlier traditions when situations demand it. A rich man's mother, or the kind of mother he may wish he had, will have a lot in common with the accepted models of forty or fifty years ago, and the man himself will be reassured by catching an occasional glimpse of it in you.

How should you comport yourself in rich company? Be interested, but not overly inquisitive; impressed, but not intimidated; ingenuous but not imbecilic. In short, always choose the middle road, but be versatile while traveling that road and always like yourself. It's simple, but not easy.

A rich man will enjoy showing you his world and watching your reactions, but only if those reactions are genuine. When you feel out of your depth, rely on him to pull you out of it. Teaching you something new or providing you with out-of-the-ordinary (and out-of-your-budget) experiences may give him more pleasure than anything else.

Beyond the fundamentally proper forms of decorum, you should cultivate one basic attitude when dealing with a rich man: generosity. Most people view the rich as an opportunity to obtain something they want: a trip on a yacht, a ringside seat or an invitation to a black-tie ball. Rich people detect all forms of opportunism, and

RECOMMENDED READING FOR ANTIQUES, ARCHITECTURE AND THE ARTS

Antiques:
Books: *Kovels' Know Your Antiques* by Ralph M. Kovel and Terry H. Kovel
Magazines: *Antiques*
Art & Antiques

Architecture/Interior Design:
Books: *A Visual Dictionary of Architecture* by Francis D. K. Ching
A History of Architecture: Settings and Rituals by Spiro Kostof and Gregory Castillo
The History of Furniture: Twenty-five Centuries of Style and Design in the Western Tradition by John Morley
Magazines: *Architectural Digest*
Home Decor
Frame

Art:
Books: *The History of Art: The Western Tradition* by H. W. Janson and Anthony F. Janson
Magazines: *ARTnews*
Art in America
Art & Antiques

Dance:
Books: *Ballet 101: A Complete Guide to Learning and Loving the Ballet* by Robert Greskovic
Ballet Book: Learning and Appreciating the Secrets of Dance by American Ballet Theater and Nancy Ellison

Ballet and Modern Dance: A Concise History by
   Jack Anderson
Magazines: *Dance*

Music:
Books: *Classical Music 101: A Complete Guide to
   Learning and Loving Classical Music* by Fred Plotkin
100 Great Operas and Their Stories by Henry W.
   Simon
Jazz: A History of America's Music by Geoffrey C.
   Ward and Ken Burns
Magazines: Stick with the books, as there really
   aren't any general music magazines or those that
   cover classical or opera—which are likely to be
   the musical areas of interest to your wealthy friends.

10 TOP U.S. SHOPS
FOR WOMEN'S FASHION

Stop in and buy a piece or look for the labels in resale shops.

Fred Segal, Los Angeles, CA
Melrose Avenue high-fashion mecca for stars du jour

Riley James, San Francisco, CA
The city's "It" girls flock to this colorful
boutique for the latest in fashion

Base, Miami Beach, FL
Designer Steven Giles redefines
South Beach style at Miami Beach store

Mitzi and Romano, Atlanta, GA
Racks upon racks of current style with
an irresistible accessories counter

Krista K, Chicago, IL
Feminine meets urban at buzzy, Lakeview boutique

Hemline, New Orleans, LA
Hip franchise and granter of easy access
to runway fashions

Wish, Boston, MA
The store that could make all your
trendy design dreams come true

Jill Anderson, New York, NY
Simple, timeless, well-made designer
clothes for downtown divas

Lena Medoyeff Studio, Portland, OR
Luxury meets simple, elegant style
in Portland designer's digs

Me & Blue Boutique, Philadelphia, PA
Fashion finds make this boutique worth
the climb to an upstairs space

WEB SITES FOR RESALE OF COUTURE CLOTHING

Dress your best without high-end consignment shops in your area.

Shop on-line for Armani Black Label, Bainan, Bes-Ben, Dior, Dolce & Gabbana, Ferragamo, Gucci, Hermès, Jimmy Choo, Kate Spade, Judith Leiber, Manolo Blahnik, Louis Vuitton, Moschino, Norell, Prada, Pucci, St. John, Valentino, etc.

www.thesnob.com
www.ritzconsignment.com
www.jillsconsignment.com
www.turnaboutshoppe.com

their harsh reaction to those who are covetous and manipulative is at the root of their reputation for parsimony. If you use a rich admirer like a lever for prying open the heavy lids of luxurious troves, he will undoubtedly react with meanness, adamantly slamming

those lids on your fingers. But if you are generous in spirit and embrace even the smallest pleasures while patiently enduring any inconvenience, he will react with attentive kindness and perhaps endure any inconveniences that arise on your end.

Many women who are being courted by a rich man are surrounded by a palpable aura of insecurity. Such women are extremely offhanded about even the most special experiences or gifts. They disdain anything ordinary and treat the finest as their due. This type of woman exhausts and bores men. You should avoid at all costs adopting the mannerisms of these ersatz rich women. No matter how insecure or intimidated you feel, you must never react negatively. Always be open and appreciative rather than defensive and difficult.

Be complimentary about an unusual car, a large yacht, a mannerly butler or a marble palace, but also never act as if it's the only one you've ever seen or, even worse, compare it to the one your mythic Aunt Shirley has in Hoboken. Learn to enjoy nice, luxurious or even overly large things simply because they are fun, comfortable or convenient, not because you know they cost a lot.

On the other hand, you should be prepared to find pleasure in the ordinary as the rich often do. For many of them, the plain, the cheap or the shoddy are all entirely extraordinary. A Big Mac may have the same exotic appeal for a rich man that Chateaubriand may have for you. So, if your rich prince suddenly veers through

better than something expensive yet ubiquitous. When giving gifts among themselves, the rich usually have an impeccable sense of the appropriate. They are practiced in the art of thoughtfulness to a degree that enables them to find just the trinkets and trifles that gratify a friend's individual taste. Give him something that shows how well you understand him rather than some overblown testament to the high hopes you are placing on his affections. Perhaps you can find an old copy of his favorite children's book, or buy him a month's supply of the freshly ground coffee he can't live without. The secret of giving presents to the rich is neither the luxury nor rarity of the item, but good taste. It is truly the thought that counts.

When you express gratitude for a gift or compliment, "Thank you" is always correct but you can also reply with "You're sweet" or "Aren't you sweet?" or "I'm flattered" for a compliment, and "You're sweet to be so thoughtful" and "I'm touched" for a gift.

New money is often at the root of dubious and extravagant purchases, the crude evidence of which flourishes in every quarter. Intoxicated by the thrill of his splendid ascension, a newly rich man will litter his home, office, yacht with examples of his new ability to purchase things of quality and beauty. Unfortunately, these items are often bought in some haste and, in his intention to own what is considered "hot" and in style at the moment, the unrestrained man with money may realize only the grotesque. He will accomplish, at a high price, only a grandiose statement of his own lack of culture and his craving to appear suave; he will be ridiculed by many as a spendthrift and by others as a boor. While some men get lost in the glare of their own gaudy surroundings, the fear of such ridicule is great in others, who realize that spending money like madmen does not ensure that their purchases reflect taste as well as wealth. It will occur to many such rich men that a woman of cultivated sensibilities could be of invaluable assistance. You must, in such predicaments, be ready to jump into the fray and help by asserting your own good taste.

Although your opportunities to exercise tasteful style in a material way have probably been heretofore restricted by financial limitations, that does not mean you don't already have an impeccable sense of the appropriate. Good taste isn't a characteristic that is exclusive to only the old rich, but before you can take part in the quiet little dramas in which the upper class places its refined sensibilities on display, you must familiarize yourself with the stage, the props, the costumes and the lines. In other words, you will most likely need to know about architecture, period furniture and the fine arts, and have a working knowledge of the exotic vocabularies that give reference to them.

Many excellent books have been published on the finer points of architecture, art and furniture, and they can certainly provide you with the necessary jargon to sound knowledgeable about each area. In fact, the reading may actually help you become more articulate when talking about houses and their contents than the people who own them. Wealthy people often know what looks right because they have been living with fine things since they first emerged from the nursery. They won't always, however, understand the extraordinary details of Great-Grandmother Fortesque's bonnet-topped highboy in any greater depth than you might comprehend the high-tech circuitry of the wide-screen television that Uncle Ralph laid on your folks after he won at the track.

The fine-arts section of any library contains a huge number of books about architecture, furniture and the arts. Be sure to look through some on Early American houses and antiques. After the library, it would also help to spend some time in museums and antique shops. You will probably have learned enough from your reading to ask intelligent questions, and curators and shop owners are usually delighted to share knowledge with someone who is genuinely interested.

Preferences and pronouncements in the realms of music, painting and literature should be displayed only if you are well educated in a particular area. People with real understanding of the fine arts usually speak little. You are more apt to appear knowledgeable and tasteful by presenting an appearance of keen interest and remaining quiet than you are by speaking erroneously, even briefly.

Clothing

Learning enough to converse with intelligence about architecture and the arts can be accomplished easily; a specific familiarity with more exotic areas such as automobiles, boats and horseflesh is helpful, but not really necessary. Clothing, of course, is a different matter. Talk is not enough where clothes are concerned. Your general taste will be judged by what you wear. In addition, how you dress signals to the world how you expect to be treated. Underdressing or overdressing marks you as a person without taste or breeding (the same theory applies to cosmetics and hair).

You should have at least one key piece of clothing and anchor accessory. Understated Tiffany or Cartier tank watches aren't that expensive but definitely signify quality. A Mont Blanc pen isn't quite enough but stick it in a Chanel bag and you're on your way. You may discover that the more effort you put into your personal style, the more effortless it seems to others. You'll be amazed at how fast an outfit will come together when you have a really nice piece or two.

The fashion industry has pumped up fashion-conscious women into such a frenzy of mindless consumption that an objective point of view on what is truly tasteful is difficult to attain. A woman who reads even a few of the fashion magazines is tugged in a thousand irrational directions by a desperate bombardment of sales hype from fashion designers, advertisers and editors alike. To find your way through the morass you must remain calm; remember that the emphasis placed on the alleged shortcomings of your wardrobe is only a marketing ploy, and one that you must avoid falling for.

Don't accede, with every turn of the fashion page or each step down a splendor-laden aisle, to the neurotic cravings of standard mall shoppers or the nouveau riche. Think of observing, not buying. Try to adopt the attitude of the old rich: if you don't have it, it's probably not worth owning. Read the magazines and visit the shops as an enjoyable way of observing an interesting industry, but wear only what is right for you in style and size, as well as those pieces that genuinely reflect your personality. Be careful not to try to say too much with clothes. Bad taste is more obvious than good taste, so let understatement be the basis of your choices. All but a handful of upper-class women—a highly publicized handful—dress in a classic, somewhat traditional manner. You will fit in more easily if you do the same. And you may even become a source of bafflement and intimidation to the status-hungry, compulsive-spending *arrivistes*.

If you want, for instance, to be treated like a queen and have dates instead of mating sessions, study slightly older women who are where you want to be in a few years, but don't completely discard those characteristics that make you unique. The beauty and mystery of a female, rich or poor, are not contrived products of exercise, cosmetic surgery or artfully applied makeup so much as a natural process that comes from within. Charm and grace can't be bought—but they can be cultivated.

Be age appropriate. For some brief, highly subjective and admittedly pricey suggestions, I've enlisted the aid of Liz Parker, who offers: In your twenties, try mixing Dior with Versace and Dolce & Gabbana. If you're north of thirty, consider investing in Gucci, Donna Karan and Prada (couture, if possible). Over forty is the time for Armani, Jaeger, Chanel and Burberry's.

If your funds are limited, there are resale shops in large cities that specialize in only couture designers—a great way to pick up a Chanel bag or Jaeger jacket. Do some homework to determine what, with a working girl's budget, would be the perfect one or two pieces of clothing and single can't-live-without accessory for you. Which would be too gaudy or false? Which should you *never* wear (fake diamonds, beads, etc.)? Simple, elegant clothes and jewelry don't have to cost a fortune. You'll be amazed at what can be found at Marshall's, Target and T. J. Maxx!

But if you can, do try to splurge on one classic, expensive item that you wear (or have with you) at all times. Not only will it show that you have class, but it will also give you more confidence as you mingle with those who can afford ten of a particular piece. The theory here is that having one is better than having none. A Chanel bag is always appropriate. A string of eight-millimeter pearls can be worn with everything but a

swimsuit. And diamond studs can be worn with everything.

Health, Fitness and Looking Young

Exercise and eat right. This may sound obvious, but
it really is so key when looking for a rich husband. Men
with money usually feel they are entitled to the best,
and as we all know, in this day and age, being fit and
healthy and looking young are part of what makes
someone "the best." Unfortunately, beauty can often be
expensive. If money is tight, do what you can at home
(workouts with videotapes or DVDs, manicures, home-
made or store-bought masks, etc.) while leaving the
tricky (and physically impossible to do yourself) tasks
to the experts (haircuts, waxing, massages, etc.). Or if
you're nervous about performing any of these proce-
dures at home, they can all be had for cheap by going to
your local beauty school, where they will be done by
a student. If you can afford expensive makeup les-
sons, great. If not, try going to counters that give free
makeovers and advice (although be forewarned: they do
usually pressure you to buy products). And read the
women's magazines—they're full of great, inexpensive
tips regarding health, fitness and skin care.

The key, of course, is staying healthy and living a
balanced life. Healthy living increases productivity and
decreases stress levels. Exercise every day. Replace cof-

fee with black tea; you'll be less nervous. Drink a lot of water; it curbs appetite and keeps your energy up.

Most important, always keep in mind that a good life is achieved through more than just a great body and fabulous looks. If you're leading a healthy, satisfying life, it will be evident in all you do. And that is bound to help you catch a rich man.

TARGET PROFILE
The Artist/Creative Type

Age: 31
Height: 6'
Weight: 181 lbs.
Interests: Boxing, ballet and chess
Net Worth: $5.1 million

A rare specimen, the Artist/Creative Type is also a chronic social critic, ever ready to take a position.

If you crave creativity and originality, this is your man. Our surprisingly wealthy abstract expressionist offers financial security to any woman willing to endure his obstreperous nature.

Nag not.

The Artist/Creative Type sample Q&A

Q. *Why are you still single?*
A. Like Groucho once said, "I'd never join any club who would have me as a member."
Q. *What is your type?*
A. The coldhearted ghetto girl who sees an evil scheme in every move I make. I love those tough broads from working-class urban backgrounds.
Q. *Under what circumstances would you marry?*
A. When I succeed in melting the heart of a nicotine-saturated, inner-city man-hater.
Q. *How long have your previous relationships lasted?*
A. Until I've fallen apart.

Q. *Do you engage in more than one relationship at the same time?*
A. No. Mine are too intense.
Q. *How do you meet women?*
A. At AA meetings and municipal gyms.

Food & Cooking

This I set down as a positive truth.
A woman with fair opportunities and
without positive hump may
marry whom she likes.
—William Makepeace Thackeray

Food: it's the great equalizer. Everyone has to eat, most people love to eat, and you don't have to be rich to put together a great meal.

The importance of food and cooking in courtship cannot be overemphasized. Food is often used as a show of endearment, and as is the case with songs, certain foods bring back all kinds of memories for all kinds of people.

Cooking for someone brings this one step further—the act itself shows that you feel that the object of your attention is worth the time and energy it takes to put a single recipe or meal together. But if you can't cook, fear not. As long as the choice of food (either bought prepared or cooked with your own hands) shows how much you're interested in someone, and is likely to create fond memories later on in the relationship, you'll be fine.

SUCCESS STORY

"Our kids brought us together," says tall, capable Wendy, who at thirty-five went to work as a squash pro at a local racquet club. "Racquet work landed me the job that helped keep my son Jake in private school."

At a school soccer match, her son bowled over the son of a building magnate from Boston. She cheered while he groaned, before they looked at each other and laughed. Later, over postgame punch, they laughed some more and decided to picnic at Crane's Beach with the boys the following Sunday.

"Tony was a widower and devoted to his son. He wanted Paul to have better schooling than he had himself so the youngster wouldn't have to follow him into the construction business. Tony certainly had the money to give his son a start anywhere, but he knew it would take more than that. At first he liked Jake, my son, because he saw a nice refined friend for Paul. But now, the way it's worked out, I think we've all enriched each other's lives in many, many ways."

You would agree if you could see them all together. When each school year is over, they spend their summers as a happy family in their place on Cape Cod.

There are of course numerous opportunities to include food and cooking in the courting process: attentive, imaginative meals with fresh fruit centerpieces, a single orchid in a bud vase, simple place settings in a mixture of wood and pewter, and bright linen napkins and colorful place mats or tablecloths are all excellent alternatives to the standard white linen napkin and china-laden table. Picnics can be grand cloth napkin and candlelit celebrations on your living room floor. On the more lighthearted side, there are tailgate parties at Ivy League football games, dining on the beach, or even hot dogs and beer in his box seats at a Major League Baseball game.

Here are a few recipes that have helped women bag their rich men, with an explanation of why they worked.

Patricia's Pasta Puttanesca

"This is a passion plate of spaghetti with capers, olives, tomatoes and hot peppers," Patricia advises with a sly smile. "The man I was seeing at the time was from an Italian family and loved spicy food, so I took an Italian cooking class just to learn how to make it."

¼ cup extra-virgin olive oil

2 2-oz. cans flat anchovy fillets cured in salt or olive oil and minced

6 plump fresh garlic cloves, minced

½ tsp. crushed red peppers (hot red flakes) or to taste

Sea salt

1 28-oz. can peeled Italian plum tomatoes in juice or crushed tomatoes in puree

20 salt-cured black olives, such as Italian Gaeta or French Nyons olives, pitted and halved.

3 tbs. capers, drained and rinsed

1 pound dried Italian spaghetti

1 cup fresh flat-leaf parsley leaves, chopped

In an unheated skillet large enough to later hold the pasta, combine the oil, anchovies, garlic, crushed red peppers and a pinch of salt, stirring to coat with oil. Cook over moderate heat until garlic turns golden brown but not crispy, 2 to 3 minutes. Add tomatoes directly from the can, crushing them by hand if they're whole. Add olives and capers. Stir to blend and simmer, uncovered, until the sauce begins to thicken, about 15 minutes, while tasting for seasoning.

Meanwhile, in a large pot, bring 6 quarts of water to a roiling boil. Add 3 tablespoons of salt along with the spaghetti, stirring to prevent sticking. Cook until tender firm to the bite. Drain thoroughly.

Add the drained pasta to the skillet with the sauce.

Toss, cover and let it rest off the heat for 1 to 2 minutes to allow the pasta to absorb the sauce. Add the parsley and toss again. Transfer to warmed shallow soup bowls and serve immediately.

This recipe will yield six servings and should be served with a dependable Chianti, such as one from the Antinori or Ricasoli estates.

Deb's Marinated Swordfish

Deb, who looks like a sex goddess but once had trouble cooking anything more complicated than the basics, says, "Food is important in landing the right guy, and certain types of dining can be wonderfully romantic. I wasn't always a great cook but wanted to do something classy the first time my husband-to-be came to my house for dinner, so this easy main course is what I cooked."

2 lbs. swordfish steaks
Juice of one lemon
2 tbs. extra-virgin olive oil
4 large cloves of garlic finely chopped
2 tsp. or less finely chopped fresh rosemary

Mix all ingredients in a shallow dish and marinate 20–30 minutes. Grill swordfish steaks over hot coals for about 4 minutes per side while basting with marinade.

Serves 4 with Mango Salsa (p. 80).

Deb's Mango Salsa

1 ripe mango diced
Juice of one fresh lime
½ sweet red pepper diced
1 small red pepper diced
2 tbs. chopped cilantro
1 tbs. chopped fresh jalapeño
2 dashes of Melinda's Hot Sauce
Salt and fresh ground pepper to taste

Mix all ingredients together. Let sit for a few hours,
if possible. Produces 1½ cups of tangy salsa that can be
kept in refrigerator for 3 days. Should be served with a
crisp white Burgundy such as those from the Louis La-
tour or Pierre Amiot estates.

Goody's Chocolate Seduction

*"I found out that this was my husband's favorite as a kid and
served it one evening well into our relationship," says Goody.
"It did the trick—he proposed after dessert that night."*

**1 package (18 oz.) Duncan Hines chocolate
cake mix**
1 tsp. cinnamon
1 cup Hellmann's mayonnaise

1 cup water
3 eggs

Preheat oven to 350°. Spray two 9-inch pans with cooking spray and coat with flour. In a large mixing bowl, stir cake mix and cinnamon until mixed. Then add mayo, water and eggs and beat on low speed for 30 seconds, then medium speed for 2 minutes. Pour batter into prepared pans.

Bake 30 minutes. Cool pans on wire racks.

Goody's Buttercream Frosting

1½ sticks soft butter
2½ cups 10x confectioner's sugar
Pinch of salt
2 tsp. vanilla
2–4 tbs. milk

Combine all and beat for several minutes until nice and smooth and creamy. Add milk judiciously—you want the frosting to be spreadable, but not runny. May be served with a velvety ruby port such as those from Fonseca or Taylor Fladgate.

Keep in mind that food can be very sexy as well as romantic. Remember the kitchen scene in the movie *9½ Weeks?* Need I say more?

TARGET PROFILE
The Small-Business Owner

Age: 46
Height: 6'1"
Weight: 192 lbs.
Interests: Racquetball and flying his own plane
Net Worth: $22.7 million

He did it himself.

This entrepreneur is a rough-and-ready guy with a lot of money that he doesn't know how to spend well—yet. If you are inventive enough to slow him down, and show him how to spend his money properly, he will be grateful.

Do not try to tame him though. He likes excitement. He will always want to make the most of every moment of every day, and he will never have tolerance for the airs of high society, or for people who make class distinctions.

Look provocative for him. The ultratailored look or conservative elegance is wasted here. Instead, try outfits that show just a bit more skin. But keep it in check. Even for this type of man, not overdoing it is the key.

The Small-Business Owner sample Q&A

Q. *Why are you still single?*
A. The right girl hasn't come strolling along, and I've been too busy to go looking for her.
Q. *What is your type?*
A. A great big beautiful doll who knows how to act like a lady. I date a lot of models and European girls.

Their backgrounds really couldn't matter less to me. I like them because they're daring in the way they look and dress. They have more dash, I think, than ordinary girls. I do admit to enjoying the ripple I cause when I walk into, say, Lutèce with a lot of glamour on my arm. But it's not just image. When I was a kid, we were poor, the gray and the unattractive surrounding me in a world I never want to go back to. It really makes me feel alive to be with a bright and cheerful woman who knows what she wants, where she's going and who she wants to go there with.

Q. *Under what circumstances would you marry?*

A. When I can't bear to spend another day without her.

Q. *How long have your previous relationships lasted?*

A. Most of them are still going on.

Q. *Do you engage in more than one relationship at the same time?*

A. I'll put it this way: only one per port.

Q. *How do you meet women?*

A. If I'm attracted, I walk up and introduce myself.

The Secrets of Rich Sex

Nothing prepares a couple for coupling like the violin.
—Kevin Doyle

You may never again be taken to the rapturous heights you experienced with that intense but penniless playwright or the macho engineer who looked so good in tight jeans. You have, however, chosen your new course, so here's some insight into the sexual habits of the upper class.

There is one general truth about rich men and sex: rich men are usually experienced. They have enough leisure time and resources to spend time with many attractive women, and those women have the good sense to sleep with them.

The kinds of sexual activities a rich man prefers are as varied as they are for any other man. Among the rich there is a broad range that tends more toward the erotic, as opposed to the working class, who tend to be more romantic. What distinguishes a rich man in bed is that

10 TOP FOURTH-DATE
RESTAURANTS IN U.S.

Fleur de Lys, San Francisco, CA
Redefines the extreme art of luxurious French dining

Il Cielo, Beverly Hills, CA
Lush, twinkling Italian courtyard is
the epitome of L.A. seduction

Manor House Restaurant, Littleton, CO
Famous Georgian-style mansion with sweeping
views and excellent continental cuisine

Tantra, Miami Beach, FL
Erotic cuisine and exotic atmosphere
make dining a feast for all the senses

Meritage, Atlanta, GA
Buckhead restaurant in romantic setting
with rich Mediterranean classics

Geja's Café, Chicago, IL
Fondue hideaway is the perfect
prelude to a passionate evening

Bella Luna, New Orleans, LA
Fine dining and romance
overlooking the Mississippi River

Savoy, New York, NY
Intimate foodie's delight on
a forgotten corner of SoHo

Ristorante Fratelli, Portland, OR
Luscious Italian fare and warm,
lustrous, unpretentious ambience

Reed's Jazz & Supper Club, Austin, TX
Upscale elegance with creative cuisine, nightly jazz
and first-rate wines and well-crafted cocktails

he knows exactly what he likes because he has had plenty of opportunities to experiment and indulge his appetites.

The lack of sexual inhibitions among the rich is well documented. Most tales of orgiastic escapades are set in the palaces of earlier times or in the posh resorts and luxurious homes of the present day. There is an underpinning of money and leisure to almost any tale of erotic coupling you have read or heard about or could even dream about. Beautiful girls writhing on gigantic platters of glistening caviar or splashing in ticklesome tubs of bubbly champagne are not doing their writhing and splashing in walk-up apartments or mobile homes. They may be doing plenty of other things in the shabbier part of town, but those pleasures usually involve romance, not erotica. If you are more interested in tender love affairs than tantalizing sex, you are heading for the wrong side of town.

The psychological basis for a rich man's lack of sexual inhibition may be simply stated. His attitude toward sex is merely an extension of his other appetites: when he wants something, he believes he deserves it. He doesn't agonize about the expense or worry about neglecting someone else in favor of his own pleasures. He simply reaches out and amiably helps himself to whatever he wants. If he wants some cherries on his salmon, he will ask for some. If he would like the Jacuzzi filled with maple syrup, that will be arranged as well. And if he has an impulse to see how you might look standing on your head with a pumpkin between your knees, you can expect a direct request. Soon.

Of course, what actually happens between you and a rich lover in bed will depend on the chemistry between the two of you rather than on the availability of pumpkins. The best way to assure that the chemistry will be explosive is to be relaxed and responsive. Rich men are accustomed to wielding authority. People jump or roll or bounce on command in a manner just as readily as a conscientious butler stoops to remove a rich man's galoshes. This does not mean that servility in the bedroom is always preferred or that a submissive role will be assigned to you. It only means that the word "no" is unfamiliar to a rich man's ears, and it would probably be abnormally off-putting to hear it whispered in bed. More important in bed than fancy tricks, pert rambunctiousness or semihysteric verbosity is a friendly attitude of willing cooperation, the kind of willing consideration he has learned to take for granted.

Sex is often more important to a rich man than it might be to a man of lower station. He needs something of sufficient complexity and interest with which to pleasantly occupy himself in lieu of an occupation. More fundamentally, an idle rich man requires an activity where his success can be measured, where his self-worth can be objectively demonstrated. Often, that presents itself most appealingly in the arena of his oversized, well-appointed bed. In other words, since his sexual accomplishments may be the only area where a rich man's performance can actually be measured, an unusual amount of his personal identity is at stake when your rich suitor lands you in bed. His bold self-image cannot be supported completely by the splendid figure of sartorial effulgence he presents to society. As a man without a burden to test himself, he needs to compensate for his lack of masculine activity. For the rich, sex is often just such compensation.

The need to perform well in bed is amplified by the rich man's desire to dispel the myths of diluted masculinity that have been a traditional part of his popular image. It is unusual, in actuality, for a rich man to measure up to a working man in masculine attributes. A man whose most difficult task is to stand perfectly still for his tailor for minutes at a time doesn't develop the same strength and toughness you will find in a man who spends his days swinging a hammer. In attempts to disprove this obvious truth, rich men often put on preposterous displays in the bedroom. No matter how feeble your lover is in reality, it is always wise to act impressed and even a little intimidated.

Apart from assorted flexing and posturing in the boudoir, the rich man is prone to offering proof of his masculine worth in another, even less agreeable way: by sleeping with two or more women simultaneously. The impulse to two-time his sweethearts has deep roots in other parts of the rich man's psychology separate from his need to prove masculinity and eschew femininity. Two-timing is deeply compatible with the rich man's notion that more of everything is better. A man accustomed to luxurious living will not turn down a weekend on a sailing yacht just because he has returned only the day before from a long cruise through the Greek isles. Similarly, he will not forgo an evening with a brunette just because he was rolling around with a terrific little blonde that very afternoon. A rich man will appreciate your sexual favors as much as any other man, but to relish something only in the afterthought will seem to him a little pallid. He will usually reach for more of the same; right now, thank you.

The double standard is still very much standard operating procedure among the rich, partly due to the rich man's taste for dominance and partly because the women who make up wealthy society have not made the same strides toward equality made by women in the lower strata. In recent decades lower- and middle-class women have taken the opportunity to prove themselves in the workplace. Upper-class women often decline the opportunity. As a result, rich men have maintained traditional attitudes toward them.

To gain an understanding of rich sex in a way that will make it work for you, you must see it from a rich man's perspective. For the rich, sex is not a haven, nor is it a lone pleasure in a painful world. It is simply one great pleasure in a very great life, seminal pleasure that enhances many others. It is not something apart, not something in the dark. It is woven through all his days and nights like a scarlet thread that gives a shimmering excitement to the fabric of his every activity.

Is it better after tennis and polo or before swimming and sailing? It's not that simple.

For the rich, sex is the thing. It takes the place of the necessity to live gainfully, which lends purpose to causes, which shapes routines and which directs many choices. Needless to say, the psychological environments that surround sex are never simple. Rich sex is as complex as it ever gets. Good luck.

TARGET PROFILE
The Corporate President

Age: 53
Height: 5'11"
Weight: 198 lbs.
Interests: Golf and squash
Net Worth: $15 million

This smooth, no-waves type needs a social foil and he may pick an unconventional mate to keep subordinates on edge.

Don't bother with this executive while he's a VP. Wait until he makes president. Though he may have money sooner, he won't have the leisure time to enjoy it if he's still climbing the corporate ladder. Once he *is* at the top, though, he'll be able to relax and choose his heart's desire.

Be yourself. He will rarely find a straight talker among his subordinates, and you can fill a big gap in his life.

The Corporate President sample Q&A

Q. *Why are you still single?*
A. I was married once, but my ambition ruined the marriage and since then I've avoided redeveloping that part of my life.
Q. *What is your type?*
A. The temperate type. I'm divorced, and I'm currently seeing an elementary school teacher. She's about as far from my first wife on the spectrum as one can get,

that's probably why I find her so adorable. She's a construction worker's daughter; my former father-in-law was a partner in one of the big Wall Street law firms.

Lisa is ingenuous and is a constant source of refreshment and delight. Her lack of sophistication about some things is all right with me; I like being with someone who does what she wants to. Some of her friends seem a little standoffish around me, but that's all right too. I think some of them are jealous.

Q. *Under what circumstances would you marry?*

A. If a trust could be built in which I feel secure.

Q. *How long have your previous relationships lasted?*

A. Since the divorce they seem to be seasonal.

Q. *Do you engage in more than one relationship at the same time?*

A. Rarely.

Q. *How do you meet women?*

A. When I feel one stalking, I suggest we drop the game of cat and mouse.

A Cautionary Word

Get money by fair means, if you can;
if not, get money.
—Horace (*Epistles I*)

There is no easier man with whom to have an affair than a rich one. He has all the necessary leisure and mobility, but he probably has a wife and/or plenty of girlfriends too.

If you are already seeing a married man with money, consider the possible reasons for his infidelity. Perhaps he has already accomplished what you are striving for; perhaps he has married above himself and, to reassert his manhood, he needs to conduct endless affairs with women who will energetically flatter him and be at his beck and call. If controlled by the power of his wife's money, this man will never divorce in order to marry you. As good a man as he may once have been, he is only a puppet now.

Even if a rich man has the money himself, it is likely that he will not divorce. It would cost too much to shed campaign to marry well will make your life richer, not only in dollars and stocks but in cultural experience, particularly if, regardless of the outcome, you have enjoyed the adventure.

RECOMMENDED GENERAL READING

Books:
The Rich Are Different, compiled by Jon Winokur
The Last Resorts by Cleveland Amory
The Right People by Stephen Birmingham
Slim by Slim Keith
The Official Preppy Handbook, edited by Lisa Birnbach

Web sites:
www.dailycandy.com (daily sales updates for the
    single girl in L.A. and N.Y.)
www.theknot.com (weekly sales updates for the
    prewedding set)
